To my parents, for always
believing I would shine, and to Iani,
my little big star
A.A.

First American Edition 2018
Kane Miller, A Division of EDC Publishing

First published in Great Britain by Egmont UK Limited,
The Yellow Building, 1 Nicholas Road, London, W11 4AN
Copyright © Ariella Abolaffio 2018
Ariella Abolaffio has asserted her moral rights.

For information contact:
Kane Miller, A Division of EDC Publishing
PO Box 470663
Tulsa, OK 74147-0663
www.kanemiller.com
usbornebooksandmore.com
www.edcpub.com

Library of Congress Control Number: 2017960091

Printed in Malaysia
1 2 3 4 5 6 7 8 9 10

ISBN: 978-1-61067-813-1

You Are a ☆ STAR

Ariella Abolaffio

Kane Miller
A DIVISION OF EDC PUBLISHING

The world is a **big** and varied place.
There are so many things to be and do.

Sometimes you can feel a bit lost.

But don't worry, take it slow
and try new things.

Try to find your own voice . . .

. . . and the life that suits you best.

Learn what you like doing . . .

. . . and what you don't.

Be there for others . . .

. . . but don't let anyone put you down.

Appreciate those you love.

And treat yourself nicely.

Always remember that you
are a star, and you'll soon find
your place in the world.